FUN SCIENCE EXPERIMENTS

FUN SCIENCE EXPERIMENTS WITH MUSIC

Claudia Martin
Illustrated by Annie Wilkinson

WINDMILL BOOKS

Published in 2025 by Windmill Books,
an Imprint of Rosen Publishing
2544 Clinton St.
Buffalo, NY 14224

First published in Great Britain in 2022 by Wayland

Author: Claudia Martin
Illustrator: Annie Wilkinson
Series Designer: Rocket Design (East Anglia) Ltd

Cataloging-in-Publication Data

Names: Martin, Claudia, author. | Wilkinson, Annie, illustrator.
Title: Fun science experiments with music / by Claudia Martin, illustrated by Annie Wilkinson.
Description: Buffalo, New York : Windmill Books, 2025. | Series: Fun science experiments | Includes glossary and index.
Identifiers: ISBN 9781538396520 (pbk.) | ISBN 9781538396537 (library bound) | ISBN 9781538396544 (ebook)
Subjects: LCSH: Science--Experiments--Juvenile literature. | Music and science--Juvenile literature.
Classification: LCC Q182.3 M37 2025 | DDC 507.8--dc23

Printed in the United States of America

CPSIA Compliance Information: Batch #CSWM25. For Further Information contact Rosen Publishing at 1-800-237-9932

SAFETY PRECAUTIONS

We recommend adult supervision at all times while doing the experiments in this book.

CONTENTS

Give music science a try!

Music is all about science! Whether we are playing an instrument or singing a tune, we are relying on some amazing science to make every sound.

Music is a group of sounds that are pleasing to hear. All sounds are made by vibrations, which is shaking so tiny we often cannot see it. When you tap the key of a xylophone or pluck the string of a guitar, you make it vibrate. The vibration travels through the air to your ears – and you hear a sound.

Music changes in volume, which is a how loud or quiet it is. Tapping or plucking an instrument harder makes a bigger vibration and a louder sound. Music may be composed of many different types of sounds, made using different materials, from the strings and wood of a violin to the metal of a triangle. Just as scientists experiment in a laboratory, musicians and composers experiment with sounds. They listen carefully to the results of their experiments, then change the vibrations they make to create music that is loud, quiet, beautiful, or catchy.

BECOME A SCIENTIST

Like composing music or practicing an instrument, science is not about getting everything right the first time. It is about asking questions, coming up with possible answers, then testing the truth of those answers through experiments. Just as an orchestra practices a new piece again and again, discussing different ways to make it sound just right, scientists often find that their experiments need more work. They talk to other scientists and try again.

When trying the experiments in this book, work as a team, try to predict the results, and ask yourself what would happen if you did something differently. Record your results by making a sound recording or video. Display your instruments in the classroom or at home. Look for patterns in your results and discuss with your team.

DO YOUR OWN THING

You can add your own twist to all the experiments in this book. Come up with imaginative, eye-catching ways to decorate the instruments you make. Try composing your own music to play on them.

Sugary sounds

We can find out how sound is made and travels through the air by building our own drum. Our drum is going to let us see sound in action!

You will need

- An adult to help you
- Bowl
- Plastic wrap
- Elastic band large enough to stretch around the bowl
- Sugar
- Metal tablespoon
- Metal pan or tray

1. Tear off a piece of plastic wrap large enough to cover the top of your bowl and wrap around the edges.

2. Stretch the plastic wrap tightly over the bowl.

3. Secure the plastic wrap with the elastic band, making sure there are no wrinkles in the top of the plastic.

4. Sprinkle a spoonful of sugar onto the top of the plastic.

5. Hold your metal pan or tray close to the bowl, but not touching it. Bang the metal with your spoon. How does your sugar behave? What do you think is happening? Discuss your findings with your team.

DO YOUR OWN THING

Try making your own drum set! Collect different-sized plastic containers from your household recycling. Cut the bottoms off some balloons, then stretch them tightly across the tops of your containers. Secure the balloons with elastic bands. Decorate the sides of your drums with colored paper or paint. Now bang your drums using blunt pencils!

What happened and why?

When we banged with the spoon, the sugar jumped on the plastic wrap. The sugar danced because sound waves traveled through the air, making the plastic vibrate.

When we banged the spoon against the pan, we made the pan vibrate (or shake). This made the surrounding air molecules vibrate too. Molecules are tiny groups of particles.

When a molecule vibrates, it makes the molecules that are touching it vibrate. In this way, the vibration travels through the air, in the form of a wave, a little like a wave in the ocean. Along the way, each molecule passes on a bit less energy than it received, so each molecule vibrates less than the one before. That is why sounds get quieter the farther away you are from them.

WHAT DO YOU THINK?

What would happen if we banged our spoon farther away from the bowl? What if we made a quieter sound, like dropping a pin?

When we hear a sound, it is because sound waves have traveled into our ear, to the eardrum. This is a thin flap of skin that is stretched tight like a drum, a bit like our plastic wrap. The eardrum vibrates, just as our plastic wrap did. This vibration is turned into nerve signals that are passed on to the brain, which makes sense of the sound. In our experiment, the vibrations of our plastic wrap were too small to be seen, but we know the plastic vibrated because it made our super-light sugar jump!

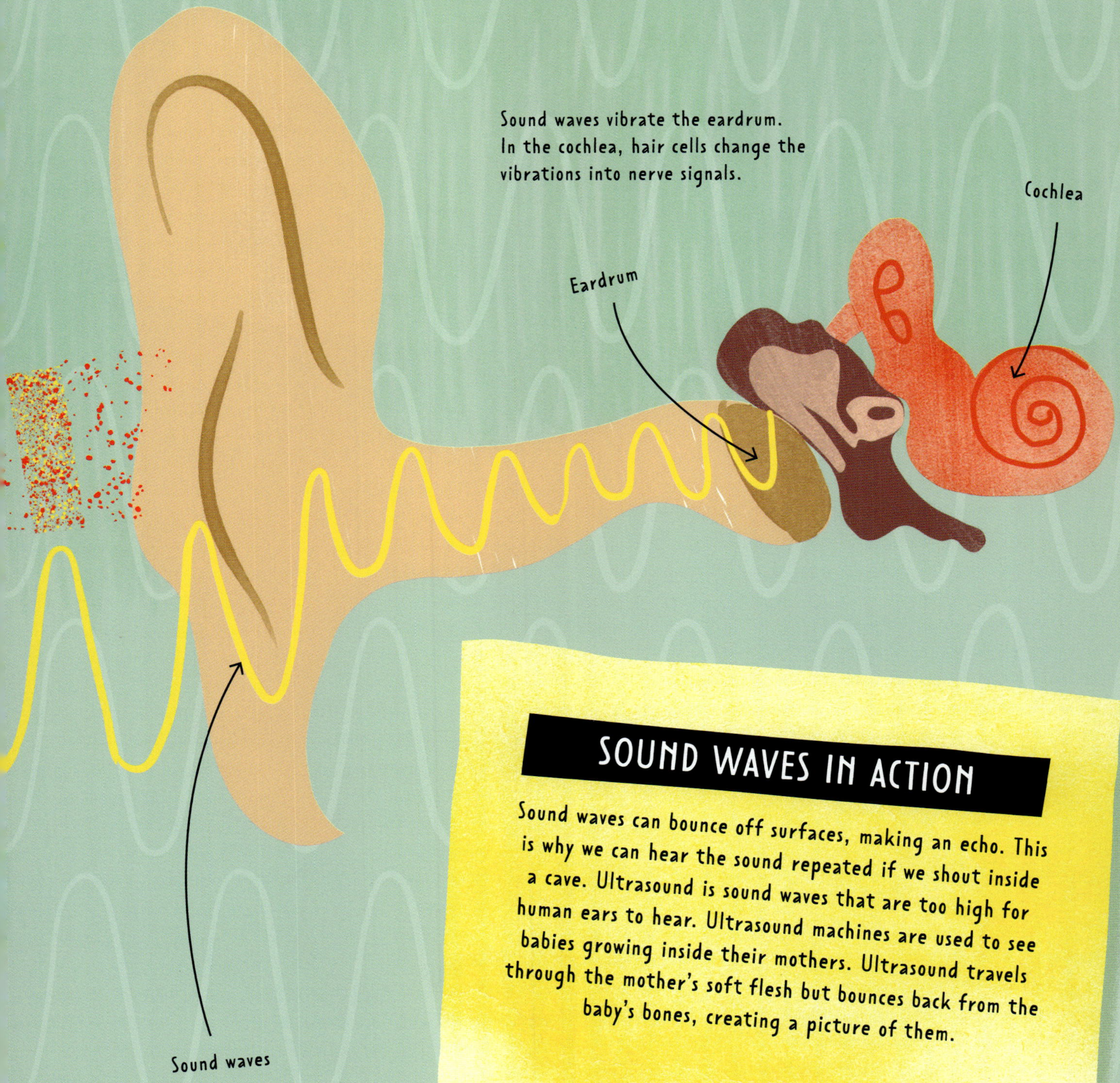

SOUND WAVES IN ACTION

Sound waves can bounce off surfaces, making an echo. This is why we can hear the sound repeated if we shout inside a cave. Ultrasound is sound waves that are too high for human ears to hear. Ultrasound machines are used to see babies growing inside their mothers. Ultrasound travels through the mother's soft flesh but bounces back from the baby's bones, creating a picture of them.

Water music

In this experiment, we will make our own magical music using glasses containing water. We are going to find out about pitch, which is how high or low a note sounds.

You will need

An adult to help you

6 identical tall, small-mouthed, thick-walled glasses

Measuring cup

Water

Metal spoons

1 Line up your 6 glasses in a row.

2 Using your measuring cup, pour 1 ½ cups of water into the first glass.

3 Now pour 1 ¼ cups of water into the second glass, 1 cup into the third glass, ¾ cup into the fourth glass, ½ cup into the fifth glass, and just ¼ cup into the last glass. You can change these quantities if needed, as long as the first glass is nearly full and the last glass is nearly empty, with the others in between!

4 Using your metal spoon, tap the side of each of the glasses in turn. Listen to the note that each glass makes.

! Be careful to tap gently so you do not break the glasses.

5 Do you notice a pattern in the sounds that your glasses make? What do you think is happening to the sound waves made by your spoon? Discuss your ideas with your team.

6 Working as a team, each with your own spoon, play a tune using your 6 glasses. You could start by figuring out how to play a well-known tune like "Twinkle, Twinkle Little Star." It is harder than you might think!

DO YOUR OWN THING

Try using your musical glasses to compose a soundtrack to a short TV or film clip. Think about using high, fast sounds to create tension, with slower, lower sounds to suggest sadness. After someone tells a joke, you could make a funny "ba-dum ching" sound effect (medium note, low note, then high note). Musicians call this funny sound effect a "sting."

What happened and why?

When we tapped the glasses that contained more water, we made sounds with a lower pitch. The pitch of a sound depends on the speed of its vibrations.

As we learned in our first experiment, sound is caused by vibrations (see page 8). When the vibrations are fast, our ears and brain hear the sound as a high pitch. When the vibrations are slower, we hear the sound as a lower pitch.

If a vibration is fast, it creates a sound wave with high frequency, which means that there is less time between the peaks of the wave. The average person can hear sounds between 20 and 20,000 hertz. One hertz is one peak per second.

WHAT DO YOU THINK?

Why do you think it is important to use 6 identical glasses in this experiment? What would happen if we used glass containers of different sizes and shapes?

When we tapped the glasses with a spoon, we made the glasses vibrate. Putting water in a glass makes it vibrate more slowly. The more water we added, the more we slowed down the vibrations of the glasses. That is why the glass that contained the most water made the note with the lowest pitch.

PITCH IN ACTION

If a glass is made to vibrate at a particular frequency, the shaking of its molecules will be so powerful that the glass will shatter. This particular frequency is called the resonant frequency. Some opera singers can sing at the correct pitch and with enough volume to shatter a glass. Never try this, or break a glass in any other way, since shattered glass is extremely dangerous!

Short straws

We will create our own wonderful wind instrument using a straw. Our instrument's sounds will be a little less musical than orchestra wind instruments — but lots of fun!

You will need

An adult to help you
Straight, tough paper straw
Scissors

1. Flatten one end of your straw.

2. Using your scissors, cut equal triangles from each side of the flattened end. In a wind instrument, this type of two-lipped mouthpiece is called a "double reed."

3 Open up the flattened end a little, then put the double reed in your mouth. Seal your lips around it – and blow. Your instrument should make a buzzing noise! If you cannot make the noise immediately, keep trying. Try closing the double reed a little so the two sides can vibrate against each other easily. Try blowing harder or softer and pressing your lips down with different amounts of pressure.

4 Listen carefully to the pitch (see page 12) of the buzzing note your instrument makes. Can you feel it vibrating?

5 Now cut 1 inch (2.5 cm) off the bottom (the opposite end from the double reed) of your instrument. Blow through it again. Has the pitch changed? Why do you think that is?

6 Repeat Step 5 two or three times. Discuss your findings with your team.

DO YOUR OWN THING

Use any leftover straws, as well as the cut sections from your experiment, to make a pan flute. Cut your straws so you have around 10 pieces, each a different length. The longest straw could be 7 inches (18 cm) long and the shortest 2 inches (5 cm). Line up the straws in height order, then join them with sticky tape. To play your pan flute, blow over the tops of your straws.

What happened and why?

When we blew into our wind instrument exactly the right way, it made a loud buzzing sound. Cutting off the end of the straw gave the sound a higher pitch.

Blowing into our instrument made the double reed vibrate. This sent waves of vibrating air down the straw. It took a few tries to make the reed vibrate at the right frequency. When we found that frequency, the air in the straw vibrated powerfully, making a buzzing noise.

WHAT DO YOU THINK?

Imagine that you had another straw, a little narrower than the one you used for your straw instrument. How could you use the second straw to change the pitch of your notes?

When we succeeded in making the buzzing noise, we found the resonant frequency for the straw, like an opera singer who finds the right frequency to break a glass (see page 13).

Every object has a natural frequency, which is a tendency to vibrate at a particular speed. When we matched that frequency for the straw, the vibrations inside the straw grew bigger. The straw resonated, which means it was filled with a loud, echoing sound – in this case, an annoying buzzing! Shortening the straw changed the length of the column of vibrating air, changing the pitch of the buzz.

WIND INSTRUMENTS IN ACTION

The oboe (pictured on the left) and bassoon are woodwind instruments played with a double reed. The mouthpiece is two pieces of cane that vibrate against each other. Players change the pitch of their sound by opening holes in the instrument using their fingers. In a single-reed woodwind instrument, such as a clarinet or saxophone, a single piece of cane vibrates against the mouthpiece.

A flute (pictured below) or pan pipe does not have a reed; the player blows air across a sharp edge, splitting the air stream to make the air in the instrument vibrate. In brass instruments, such as the trombone and trumpet, the player's lips vibrate to make the air in the instrument vibrate.

Strum a guitar

Get ready to start your own band with this homemade guitar! While you are making it, learn about how guitars play loud notes with different pitches.

You will need

An adult to help you
Rectangular plastic tub (such as an empty margarine tub)
4 elastic bands of different thicknesses
Sticky tape
Scissors
Cotton wool or bubble wrap

1 Stretch your elastic bands around your tub. Arrange them in order of thickness.

2 Use sticky tape to secure your bands to the tub so they do not slip off when you pluck them.

3 Pluck each elastic band in turn. Do they all make a note with the same pitch? Which makes a higher-pitched sound: the thickest band or the thinnest? Can you feel anything happening to the container when you pluck?

4 Reaching between the elastic band “strings,” fill your container with cotton wool or bubble wrap. Pluck your strings again. Is the sound different? Why do you think that is?

5 Working as a team, compare the sounds made by everybody’s guitars. Discuss your findings.

DO YOUR OWN THING

Do you want to make your instrument look like a real guitar? Cut a large piece of cardboard into a guitar shape, like an 8 with a fatter middle. In the middle of the 8, draw a circle around your container, then ask an adult to cut out the container hole. Use sticky tape to attach the guitar-shaped cardboard to the container. Now stick an old paper towel tube to the card to make the guitar's neck. Paint your guitar a wood color.

What happened and why?

Our guitar's thinner strings made higher-pitched notes. When we filled our container with cotton wool or bubble wrap, our guitar's music was a little quieter.

The thinner strings on our guitar make higher-pitched sounds because they vibrate more quickly than the thicker ones when they are plucked. As we learned on page 12, the faster the vibration, the higher the note we hear.

A guitar string vibrating by itself does not make a very loud sound. This is because a single string does not disturb much air. Yet our strings were attached to a hollow container. In orchestra string instruments, these hollow spaces are called sound boxes. When a string vibrates, the whole sound box vibrates at the same speed. The sound box is in contact with more air than a single string, so it moves lots of air molecules, making a louder sound.

When we filled our sound box with a material that stopped sound waves from traveling, we muffled the noise.

WHAT DO YOU THINK?

What do you think would happen if we tightened or loosened our elastic bands?

SOUND BOXES IN ACTION

Most string instruments, such as guitars and violins, have a hollow body. The vibration of the strings resonates (see pages 16–17) inside the body, making a loud echoing sound. A hole in the front of the instrument, called a sound hole in a guitar or an f-hole in a violin, allows the vibrations in the sound box to travel to the outside air. Electric guitars and violins do not have sound boxes; they use loudspeakers to make the vibration of their strings louder.

Kazoo for you

Let's make a kooky kazoo! A kazoo is an instrument that makes a buzzy noise when you hum into it. That strange sound will teach us about acoustics, the science of how sound waves travel.

You will need

- An adult to help you
- Cardboard tube from a paper towel roll
- Wax paper
- Elastic band
- Sharp pencil
- Aluminum foil

1 Cut or rip a piece of wax paper large enough to cover the end of your tube. Secure the wax paper over the end with an elastic band. Make sure the paper is tight and smooth.

2 ! **Ask for an adult's help** to use a pencil to poke a hole in the side of the tube, just below the elastic band.

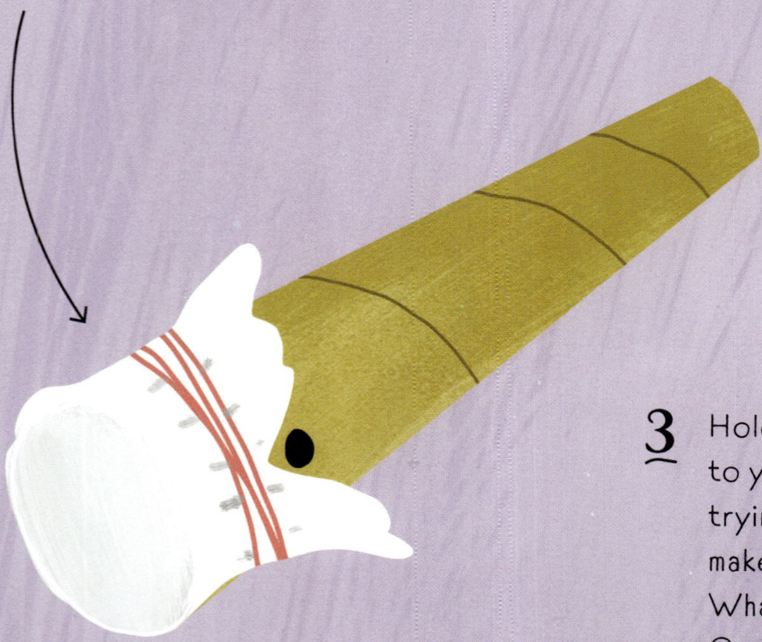

3 Hold the open end of your kazoo to your mouth, then hum. Keep trying until your kazoo starts to make your humming sound buzzy. What do you think is happening? Can you feel the tube vibrating?

4 Experiment with making different sounds. Try repeating "Boo," "Moo," or "Kazoo"! Cover or uncover the hole in the side as you do it. Discuss your results with your team.

5 ❗ **Ask an adult for help** with poking more holes in the side of your kazoo. How do those holes change the sound?

6 Now swap the wax paper for aluminum foil. Does this material work better or worse? Why do you think that is?

DO YOUR OWN THING

Decorate the outside of your kazoo with paint or felt-tip markers. You might consider bright stripes, spots, or a wobbly, rippling pattern of sound waves that are bouncing around and crossing each other!

What happened and why?

Our kazoo amplified — or made louder — the sound of our humming. It also added harmonics, which are different pitches that we hear alongside the original pitch.

When we hummed or made other sounds into our kazoo, our sound waves made the wax paper vibrate. The extra vibration amplified the sound of our voice. The sound waves from our humming also bounced around inside the cardboard tube, changing the direction and timing of how they reached our ears. This added harmonics to our sounds, making them sound strange.

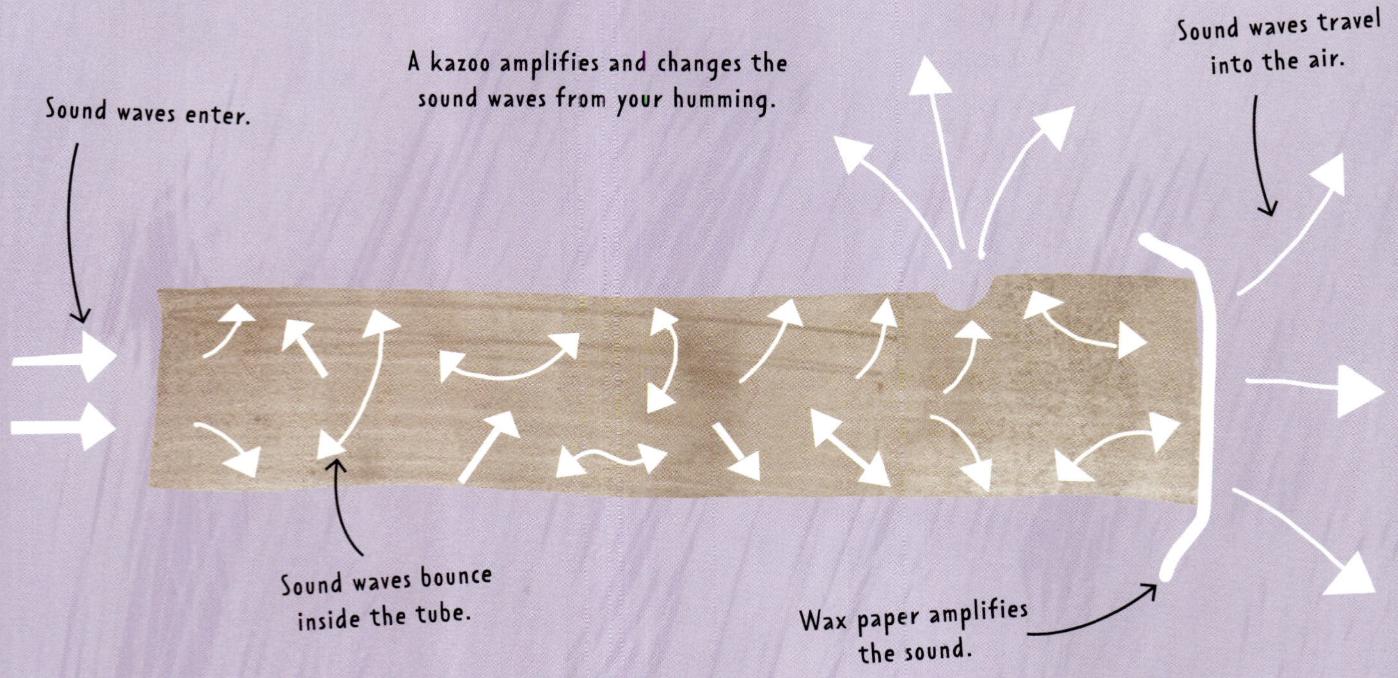

The holes in the sides of the cardboard tube allowed the sound waves to escape and reach our ears. Covering the holes made our kazoo quieter. Swapping the wax paper for foil made our kazoo less effective. The foil is stiffer than wax paper, so it did not vibrate as easily.

ACOUSTICS IN ACTION

Our kazoo showed how sound waves bouncing off surfaces can change your voice, making it sound funny! When concert halls are built, experts in acoustics design the room shape so that the sounds of singers and orchestras will not be bounced too much.

WHAT DO YOU THINK?

What do you think your kazoo would sound like if you lined the cardboard tube with cotton balls?

Sing high

Warm up your singing voice! This experiment will test vocal range, which is the highest and lowest notes we can sing comfortably. We will also find out how we make sounds when we sing and speak.

You will need

An adult to help you

Piano, keyboard, a "virtual piano" website or a free piano app downloaded to an adult's phone

Paper

Pencils

1 Gather a team that includes girls and boys, and adult men and women. However, do not worry if you cannot find every one of these people for your team since your results will still be interesting! Everyone in your team will take turns singing.

2 Find middle C on your real or virtual keyboard. On websites and apps, this key may be labeled C4. If you are not sure where middle C is, ask an adult for help.

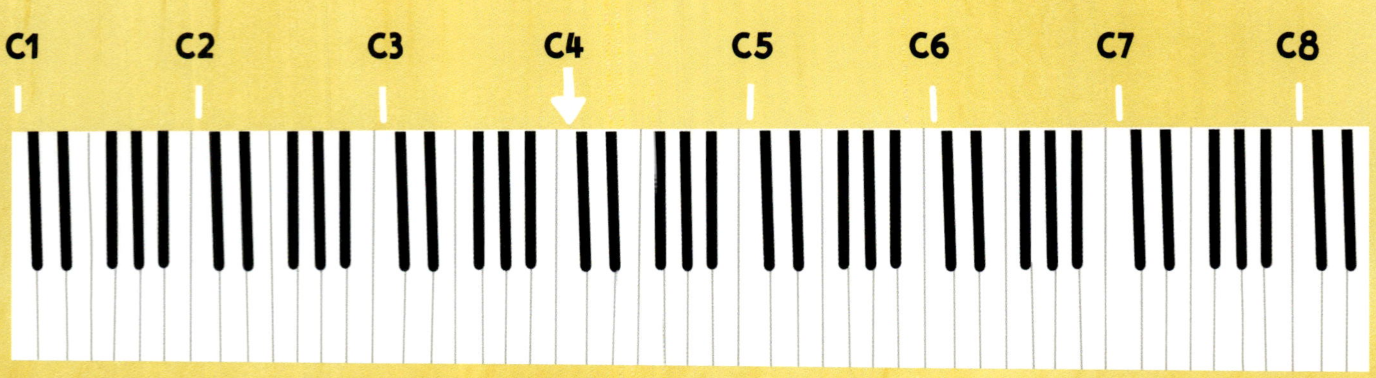

3 The keys to the right of middle C are higher in pitch, while the keys to the left are lower. We are just going to work with the white keys, which are called C, D, E, F, G, A and B, moving to the right and running in a repeating pattern. The key to the right of middle C (C4) is D4, followed by E4. Moving to the left of middle C are B3, A3, G3 and so on.

4 Play C4 for Singer 1. They should try to sing the same note. It doesn't matter if they cannot match it exactly, as most people find this difficult. Move up the keyboard, playing each note in turn, with Singer 1 trying to sing back each note. Eventually, Singer 1 will find the note too high to sing comfortably, so they will squeak or scream! This means the note is outside their vocal range. Write down the name of the last note they sing comfortably: for example, D5.

5 Now work down from middle C. When Singer 1 needs to growl to hit the note, it is outside their vocal range. Write down the last note they sang: for example, B3.

6 Repeat Steps 4 and 5 for every singer on your team.

7 Examine your results. Was everyone's vocal range similar? Did girls have higher or wider vocal ranges than boys? Were the adults' vocal ranges different? Do you have any ideas about the reasons for your results?

DO YOUR OWN THING

Using your full vocal range, compose a short, wordless song (repeating "la-la" or "me-me"). Start with a basic rhythm, then add notes that sound pleasing or catchy, using as much repetition as you like.

What happened and why?

Most children under 10 have a similar vocal range, but adult men and women have different ranges! Everyone's vocal range depends on the length of their vocal cords.

When anyone sings or speaks, they breathe out air from their lungs. The air travels up a tube called the trachea. In the throat, the air passes through the voice box (also called the larynx). In the voice box are folds of tissue called vocal cords. These vibrate as the air travels through them. As we know, vibration makes sound. When we change the pitch of the note we are singing, we are actually tightening or relaxing our vocal cords to change how fast they are vibrating. The quicker the vibration, the higher the note.

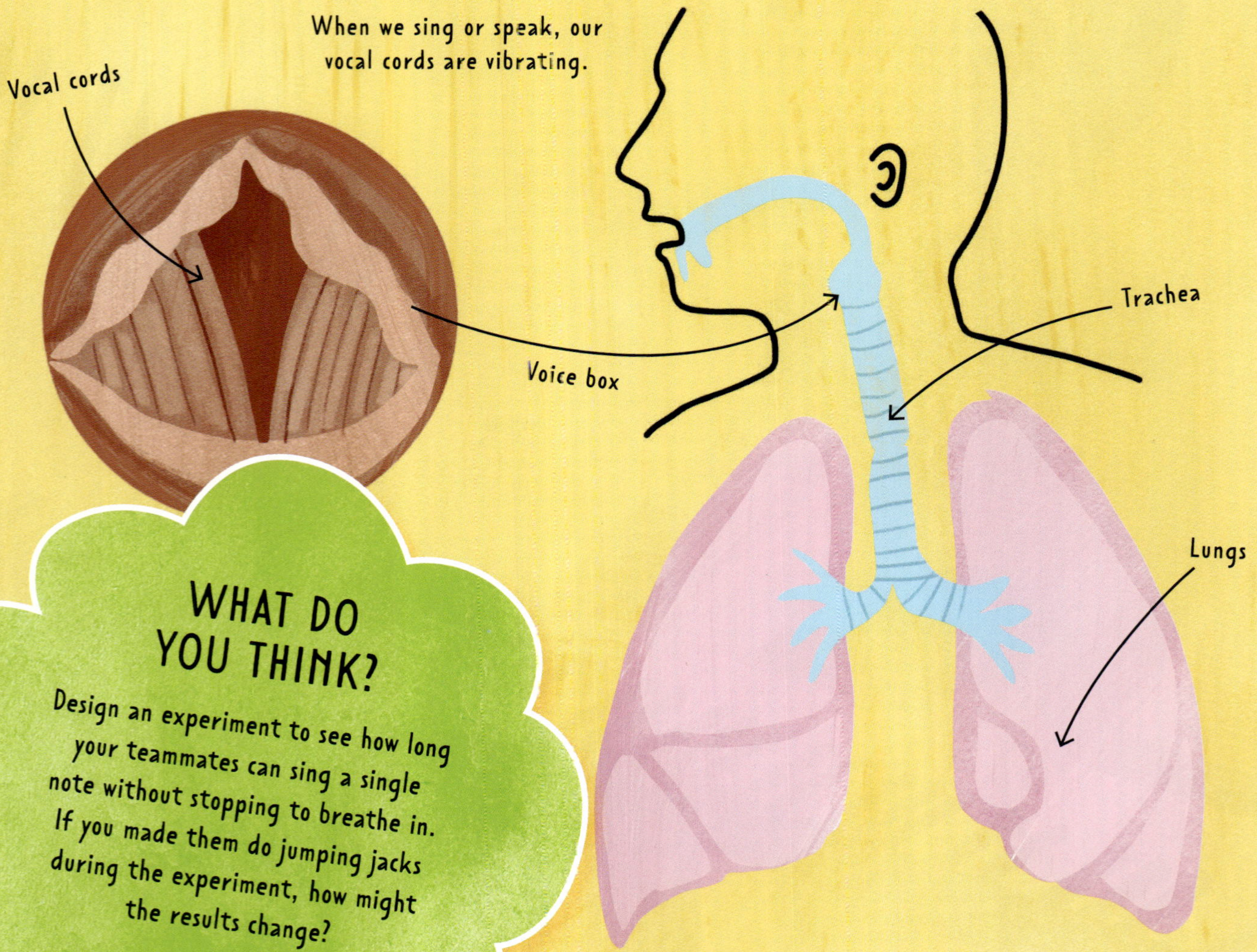

WHAT DO YOU THINK?

Design an experiment to see how long your teammates can sing a single note without stopping to breathe in. If you made them do jumping jacks during the experiment, how might the results change?

Children have short vocal cords. Shorter vocal cords vibrate faster, giving a higher voice. In children, vocal range is high and usually quite narrow. As children go through their early teens, their vocal cords lengthen. Boys' vocal cords lengthen the most, giving men lower voices than women.

VOCAL RANGE IN ACTION

The voices of opera singers are given names that describe their vocal range. The highest female voice is soprano. A soprano can sing from C4 to C6 or higher. Below that are mezzo-soprano and contralto, the lowest female voice. Male voices run from tenor – the highest, but below contralto – through baritone to bass. A bass can sing E2 to E4.

Glossary

acoustics the study of sound and vibration

amplify to increase the volume of a sound, making it louder

brass instrument a musical instrument made of brass or another metal that is played by the player's lips vibrating against a funnel-shaped mouthpiece

eardrum a drumlike flap of tissue that vibrates when sound waves pass into the ear

frequency a measure of the number of peaks of a sound wave per second

harmonics different notes heard alongside a main note

middle C a note near the middle of the piano keyboard

molecule a group of atoms that are bonded together; an atom is the smallest part of anything that can exist on its own

opera a play in which most of the words are sung alongside an orchestra; operas were first performed in Italy in the 16th century

pitch the highness or lowness of a note, with higher notes having a higher frequency

reed a thin blade of cane or metal that, in a wind instrument, is vibrated by the player's breath

resonate to fill with a rich, deep sound

sound box a hollow chamber that forms the body of a string instrument

sound wave a vibration of molecules that travels through air or water in the form of a wave and can be heard as sound

string instrument a musical instrument that is played by vibrating, plucking, or drawing a bow across strings

trachea a tube that stretches from the throat to the lungs

vibrate to move quickly to and fro

vocal cords folds of body tissue in the voice box that vibrate as air passes through from the lungs

vocal range the distance between the highest and lowest notes that a human voice can sing

volume the loudness or quietness of a sound

woodwind instrument a musical instrument, today made of wood or metal, that is played by blowing across a narrow hole (as in a flute) or by vibrating a reed (as in an oboe or clarinet)

Further reading

BOOKS

Sound (Boom! Science),
Georgia Amson-Bradshaw (PowerKids Press, 2020)

Sound (Moving Up with Science),
Peter Riley (Franklin Watts, 2020)

Spectacular Light and Sound (Extreme Science),
Rob Colson and Jon Richards (Gareth Stevens, 2024)

The Story of Music,
Mick Manning and Brita Granström (Frankin Watts, 2020)

WEBSITES

Find out more about music, instruments, and sound waves on these websites:

https://kids.britannica.com/kids/article/music/399978

www.bbc.co.uk/bitesize/topics/zgffr82

https://www.pbs.org/video/sound-the-science-of-sound-syzigq/

https://lpo.org.uk/digitalresource/improvised-instruments-the-science-of-sound/

Index